DATE DUE

DEMCO 38-296

KUNG FU AND TAI CHI

by Ann Heinrichs

Content Adviser: Philip S. Porter, Founder,
United States Martial Arts Association,
Citrus Heights, California

Published in the United States of America by The Child's World®
PO Box 326 • Chanhassen, MN 55317-0326 • 800-599-READ • www.childsworld.com

ACKNOWLEDGMENTS

The Child's World®: Mary Berendes, Publishing Director

Editorial Directions, Inc.: E. Russell Primm, Editorial Director; Halley Gatenby, Line Editor;
Susan Hindman, Copyeditor; Elizabeth K. Martin and Katie Marsico, Assistant Editors;
Matthew Messbarger, Editorial Assistant; Kerry Reid, Fact Checker; Tim Griffin/IndexServ,
Indexer; James Buckley Jr., Photo Researcher and Photo Selector

The Design Lab: Kathleen Petelinsek, Design and Page Production

PHOTOS

Cover: Bob Krist/Corbis
AFP/Corbis: 10, 28; Bohemian Nomad Picturemakers/Corbis: 26; Bridgeman Art Library: 8;
Corbis: 4, 6, 17, 20; Digital Stock: 7; Getty Images: 19, 23, 24; Bob Krist/Corbis: 16; Courtesy
www.kungfumagazine.com (reprinted by permission): 12, 13, 14, 22; Tom Nebbia/Corbis: 27;
Keren Su/Corbis: 9, 11; TRBfoto/Photodisc, 1.

REGISTRATION

LIBRARY OF CONGRESS CATALOGING-IN-PUBLICATION DATA

Heinrichs, Ann.
  Kung fu and tai chi / by Ann Heinrichs.
      p. cm. — (Kids' guides)
Contents: The fighting monks—Tigers, dragons, monkeys, and cranes—Blocks, strikes,
and kicks—The supreme ultimate fist—Waving clouds, spreading wings.
  ISBN 1-59296-029-4 (lib. bdg. : alk. paper)
  1. Kung fu—Juvenile literature. 2. Tai chi—Juvenile literature. [1. Kung fu. 2. Tai chi.]
I. Title. II. Series.
  GV1114.7.H47 2004
  796.815'9—dc22   2003018077

CONTENTS

THE MANY WAYS OF WUSHU

YOU MAY NEVER HAVE HEARD OF WUSHU.

But you've probably seen **wushu** in action.

Have you ever watched Jackie Chan, Jet Li, or Bruce Lee? These **martial arts** stars thrill fans around the world. In movies such as *Crouching Tiger, Hidden Dragon* or *The Matrix*, the actors seem like fighting acrobats. Maybe you've seen shows in which Chinese people are exercising in a park. Their slow, flowing movements can almost hypnotize you.

Action movie star Jackie Chan uses kung fu in his films.

4

All these people are practicing wushu—the Chinese martial arts. As you see, there are many styles of wushu. Outside of China, the best-known styles are kung fu and tai chi. Kung fu is called a hard, or external, style. It relies on strength and athletic power. Tai chi is a soft, or internal, style, with curved, rounded movements. Its power comes from balance and timing.

While these two styles sound very different from one another, in reality, they have a lot in common. They are often called the hard and soft versions of the same art. Both have their roots in ancient Chinese **philosophy.** Both have external and internal aspects. And both rely on ideas that seem to be opposites. Take motion and stillness, for example: Even while your body is moving (as it does so much in kung fu), your mind is relaxed and still. Even when your body is still (as is common in tai chi), your mind is moving.

Now let's take a look at these ancient fighting arts.

A WORD OF WARNING

Practicing the martial arts can be dangerous—to yourself, to those around you, and to breakable objects in your home! This book is meant to be an introduction. You should train only under the watchful eye of a qualified instructor.

THE FIGHTING MONKS

YIELD AND OVERCOME;

BEND AND BE STRAIGHT.

THE HARD AND STRONG WILL FALL.

THE SOFT AND WEAK WILL OVERCOME.

These sayings don't sound very warlike, do they? How could they be combat principles? Strange as it may seem, this way of thinking is the basis for the Chinese martial arts.

This "yin and yang" symbol is used in Taoism to show the divisions and unity in life.

6

This golden statue shows the Buddha seated in a classic pose.

The sayings were written by the Chinese philosopher Lao Tzu. He founded **Taoism** in the 500s B.C. Taoism speaks of a balance between opposite forces. They are called **yin and yang.** Yin is the soft, calm force, and yang is the hard, active force. This balance is seen in nature, as in darkness and light. It's also seen in the way people behave and move.

Later, another way of thinking arrived in China—**Buddhism.** Its focus is wisdom, peace, harmony, and compassion for all beings. Buddhist **monks** lived in **monasteries.** There they studied and practiced **meditation.**

The Buddhist monk Bodhidharma believed in strength of the body and the mind.

Into this scene came a traveling monk named Bodhidharma (Da Mo in Chinese). He came from India to China's Shaolin Temple around A.D. 520. Bodhidharma hoped to teach the monks Buddhism. But he was shocked to see how weak and sickly they were. Some monks even fell asleep while meditating!

For Bodhidharma, a strong spirit, mind, and body went hand in hand. He taught the monks exercises for breathing and strength. Simple farming tools were used for both exercise and meditation. He taught the monks to use an internal energy or life force called **chi.** This same force is called *ki* in Japanese martial arts.

The Shaolin monks grew in discipline, strength, and courage. They learned that a warrior's power can come only from within. Their exercises developed into martial arts. Their farm tools became deadly weapons.

Shaolin monks such as the one shown here are students of Bodhidharma's teachings.

THE SHAOLIN LEGACY

Many Asian martial arts trace their origins back to the Shaolin Temple. In Okinawa and other parts of Japan, the Shaolin arts became karate. In Korea, they became tae kwon do. Even Japan's Zen Buddhism grew out of Bodhidharma's teachings. In Japan, Bodhidharma is called Daruma.

THE SHAOLIN MONKS WERE KNOWN FAR

and wide for their fighting skills. If the emperor needed fighters, he often called on the monks. They could fight hand to hand. They were also skilled in the use of weapons. They used the sword, the **broadsword,** the spear, the staff, and dozens of other fighting tools. Even today, students practice to master these weapons.

Some kung fu experts train to use weapons such as this crescent moon shovel.

The bright orange pants worn by Shaolin monks allow easy movement when practicing.

Hundreds of kung fu styles arose over the years. Many styles are named after animals. They're based on the way a certain animal moves and fights. The Tiger, Snake, Crane, Dragon, and Leopard styles arose in kung fu's earliest days. Popular styles today include the Praying Mantis, Monkey, and Eagle styles.

Master Tu Jin-Sheng demonstrates a typical Tiger style kung fu movement.

Let's look at some of the animal styles and how they work. A tiger in nature, for example, springs and pounces on its prey. Its sharp claws can rip and tear. In the Tiger style, the body twists and springs to make powerful attacks. The tiger-claw is a special hand technique.

A snake coils up, then strikes out quickly. This inspired the Snake style. Cranes attack with a sharp beak. Their huge, outspread wings fend off attackers. These moves made their way into the Crane styles. In Chinese mythology, dragons live in the water. The Dragon style imitates the dragon's smooth floating, sinking, and twisting motions. The Leopard style uses the leopard's speedy footwork, with short, quick kicks and strikes.

The Monkey style includes moves like a frisky monkey. If you watch this style, you can't help laughing. The person

Flexibility is important in Dragon style kung fu, as shown by Master Jack Tu.

Wing Chun is a powerful kung fu style with bold strikes, as shown by Master Benny Meng.

who is the "monkey" hops, squats, tumbles, and rolls. He scratches his head and glances quickly from side to side. These are sneaky moves. They only trick and distract the opponent.

Then the "monkey" surprises the opponent with quick strikes. The "monkey" is hard to hit, too. He darts or tumbles away from any strike.

The Drunken style works much the same way. Its moves look staggering, wobbly, and out of control. But these moves are really super-controlled. As in the Monkey style, they're a sly trick for outwitting the opponent.

A Buddhist nun invented Wing Chun style in the 1600s. She taught the art to a teenage girl, Yim Wing Chun, who then taught others. It was Bruce Lee who made this style famous. Lee began starring in kung fu movies in the 1970s. Those movies made kung fu wildly popular in the United States.

Wing Chun is powerful because it is simple and direct. There are no wasted movements. The fighter's fists are held close to the center line of the body. Elbows are kept low. Punches and kicks are delivered in a straight line to the opponent's body.

Remember—kung fu is just one division of Chinese wushu. Many modern wushu artists blend kung fu with other wushu styles. The result is awesome! That's what you see in movies such as *The Matrix* and *Crouching Tiger, Hidden Dragon.* Of course, camera tricks and hidden wires add to the effect. However, there's no mistaking the real-life skills of a great martial artist.

BLOCKS, STRIKES, AND KICKS

WHAT CAN YOU EXPECT IN A KUNG FU

class? First of all, the training hall is called the **kwoon.**
Students address the instructor as **Sifu.** Respect for the
instructor and for fellow
students is rule number one!

Classes usually begin
with stretching and other warm-
up exercises. Then students do
drills on basic techniques. They
may practice in pairs, taking
turns as offense and defense.
Students may also practice kung
fu forms. Forms are standard
routines that combine many
movements together.

All kung fu styles use the
same basic techniques—strikes,
punches, blocks, and kicks.
But to begin, it's important to

Kung fu students
in a "kwoon" have
fun while they're
learning.

master the stances, or ways of standing.

One basic stance is the horse stance. It's easy to do but
hard to hold for a long time. First, bring your fists to the sides

16

The crane stance is a way to begin many movements.

of your waist, palms turned up. Stand with your feet wider than shoulder-width apart. Bend your knees slightly and lower your body, keeping your trunk upright. Your legs will be bowed as if you are riding a horse.

The horse stance is a "springy" stance. You are not locked in place. Your body can spring up and down, or you can shift your weight from side to side. You are ready to move quickly in any direction.

The crane stance imitates the crane's habit of standing on one leg. Shift your weight to your left leg. Then raise the right knee, with the toes pointed downward. Other stances include the cat stance, the tiger stance, and the scissors or cross-legged stance.

Let's not forget the *defense* in *self-defense.* That's where blocks come in. Blocks are defensive moves. They are ways to defend against an oncoming attack.

Suppose a punch is coming toward your head. You might block that punch with a rising back-fist. That is, you raise your arm with your hand open, fingers pointing downward. The back of your hand knocks the opponent's arm away from its mark. Other blocks use the heel of the palm, the side of the hand, or the forearm.

As for punches, some kung fu styles use short, quick punches. They are best for fighting at close range. Other styles use long-arm punches. Punches are most powerful when the body turns like a corkscrew. This turning unleashes energy from the feet all the way up to the fist.

There are many ways to strike an opponent besides punching. For example, different animal styles use special hand techniques for striking. In Crane styles, the fingers are held together in a pointy form, like a crane's beak. As you can imagine, Eagle's Claw, Tiger, and Praying Mantis styles have unique hand forms, too.

The foot becomes a weapon when used in kung fu kicks.

Kicks are probably the most exciting kung fu moves to watch. Some basic kicks are the front, the side, and the ax (diagonal) kicks. In the crescent kick, the leg swings up and around in a circular pattern. For speed and power, the spinning back kick is hard to beat. It delivers a lightning-quick, whiplike blow.

Remember, though—power begins within. It's important to master physical techniques. But a calm mind is your most powerful weapon!

THE SUPREME ULTIMATE FIST

LET'S STEP BACK AGAIN IN TIME TO THE

Shaolin Temple. According to legends, Chang San-Feng was

a Shaolin monk who had mastered all the fighting styles.

However, he began to feel that these styles were too forceful. He

went away to Wudang Mountain. There he would meditate and

work on softening the forms.

Tai chi is often practiced with other students in natural settings.

One day, Chang looked out the window. He saw a snake

being attacked by a crane. Whenever the crane darted down

to attack, the snake coiled and dodged away. Again and again, the crane stabbed with its beak. And time after time, the snake escaped, only to make its own surprise attacks.

Chang studied the animals' movements. He saw that the snake's soft, coiling moves were its greatest defenses. The crane, too, fended off attacks, using its great, curved wings. Chang blended the animal movements with Taoist ideas to create tai chi.

Tai chi chuan, or simply tai chi, means "supreme ultimate fist." It can be a fighting form. But it is best known as a form of relaxation and "moving meditation." Movements are graceful and flow with the breath. As a rule, you inhale when drawing inward and exhale when stretching outward. This helps the flow of the internal energy called chi.

Chang San-Feng teachings eventually passed to the Chen family. They developed Chang's principles into Chen style tai chi—a blend of "soft" tai chi and "hard" kung fu. It combines the graceful, defensive moves of animals with quick strikes, stomping feet, and pounding fists.

The Chens closely guarded their secrets for hundreds of years. They knew their fighting style gave them a powerful advantage over opponents. The slow moves tricked an opponent into being off guard and enabled the fighter to gather energy for a surprise attack.

Master Chen Daoyun from China demonstrates the smooth, beautiful Yang style of tai chi.

Sometime in the early 1800s, Yang Lu-Chan got a job as a servant in the Chen household. He spied on the Chens and learned their fighting arts secrets. Yang developed his own variations, creating the Yang style. Yang style has very soft, flowing movements.

Tai chi passed from master to student for many generations. Some masters made such unique variations that their style was named after them. That's how the Wu and Sun styles began.

Chinese martial arts officials created the New style in 1956. This was a way to make learning tai chi easier. New style combines features of many of the traditional styles. In the United States, beginners often start with the New style's 24 Form. The 24 Form, a shortened version of Yang style tai chi, is the most widely practiced form of tai chi in the world.

Have you ever memorized a poem, a speech, or a piece of music? If so, you know how hard it is to memorize something that is long. Some tai chi forms have more than 100 moves. They can last half an hour! Luckily, many styles have both a long form and a short form. Short forms are good for performances and competitions. They keep these events from running too long!

This move from the 24 Form is called "Fair Lady Works at Shuttles."

WAVING CLOUDS, SPREADING WINGS

AS A TAI CHI STUDENT, YOU FIRST LEARN TO

relax. Your shoulders are down, not hunched up. Your knees are slightly bent, not locked. At all times, you feel your weight. It's as if you were sinking right down through the floor.

A pair of students perform "Wave Hands Like Clouds."

Tai chi and kung fu share many of the same stances. You've already learned the horse stance in Chapter Three. The cat stance is easy, too. Stand with your feet slightly apart. Bend the knees slightly while shifting your weight to the right foot. At the same time, slide your left toe forward until your pointed toe gently rests ahead of you. From the cat stance, you can make a powerful left-foot kick.

All styles of tai chi have certain standard movements. Many of the movements have beautiful names. Some are inspired by animals—White Crane Spreads Its Wings, Grasp the Peacock's Tail, and White Snake Shows Its Tongue. Some are named for activities, such as Strum the Lute. Others are inspired by the natural world, such as Wave Hands Like Clouds and Embrace the Moon.

These movements may seem sort of "dreamy." But each one has a practical side. For example, look at White Crane Spreads Its Wings. To do this movement, first follow the instructions above for the cat stance. Then curve your left arm out with your palm facing down. Your palm will rest a few inches beside your hip and slightly toward the front.

Now for the right arm. With your elbow leading the way, curve your right arm upward beside you. Bring your palm up until it rests above and beside your head, and slightly forward.

With practice, you will move your legs and arms all at the same time.

In a real-world situation, you have just done several things. Your left arm has blocked someone's kick. Your right arm has blocked a punch. You are also prepared to make a counter-kick.

All the tai chi moves work the same way. Strum the Lute locks the opponent's elbow. At the same time, your heel pins the opponent's foot in place. Wave Hands Like Clouds is a powerful move. It's a way to fend off several attackers at once!

So you see? Tai chi may seem peaceful. But for an expert, it can be very effective in self-defense. You see the combat side of tai chi even more in weapons forms. There are tai chi routines for sword, broadsword, staff, saber, and many other weapons.

Still, tai chi is best known as a graceful art and a way to a healthy mind and body. Many people tell amazing stories of tai chi's healing effects. Of course, modern medicine should be the first stop for any medical problems. But there's no doubt about the benefits of tai chi.

Ancient writings say tai chi makes you "solid as a mountain, supple as a willow, and fluid as a great river." At the very least, tai chi makes you less stressed out! It's only natural. Your mind and body stop fighting each other and live together in harmony.

Some tai chi forms use weapons such as the sword.

No matter who you are, there's a place for you in the Chinese martial arts. Whether you're young or old, male or female, there's a style that's just right for you. Why not give it a try? Check out different schools and teachers until you find a place where you feel comfortable.

Wushu is more than just self-defense or exercise. It's a great way to channel your feelings in a positive direction. You'll grow stronger, more flexible, and more confident. You'll gain self-respect—and the respect of others, too.

Kung fu is a high-flying and powerful martial art that can benefit both your body and your mind.

GLOSSARY

broadsword—a heavy sword with a broad blade that is designed for cutting

Buddhism—a belief system based on wisdom, peace, harmony, and compassion

chi—Chinese for an energy or life force that flows through the body

kwoon—a kung fu training hall

martial arts—fighting sports or skills, especially those developed in Asian lands

meditation—focusing with a still mind; usually done while sitting, but can be done in any position

monasteries—places where monks study and meditate

monks—men devoted to a spiritual life

philosophy—a way of thinking; a way of approaching the world

Sifu—a term of respect for a Chinese martial arts instructor

Taoism—an ancient Chinese way of thought

wushu—a general term for the Chinese martial arts (including more than 3,000 styles)

yin and yang—opposite forces of soft and calm (yin) versus hard and active (yang)

TIMELINE

500s B.C. Lao Tzu begins teaching Taoism in China.

about 528 B.C. Siddhartha Gautama (the Buddha) begins teaching Buddhism in India.

about A.D. **520** Bodhidharma begins teaching at the Shaolin Temple in China; his teachings become the basis of Chinese martial arts.

1200s The Shaolin monk Chang San-Feng develops tai chi; his teachings pass to the Chen family.

1600s Yim Wing Chun develops Wing Chun style kung fu.

1800s Yang Lu-Chan develops Yang style tai chi.

1900 Chinese peasants stage the Boxer Rebellion; they are called Boxers because of their kung fu skills.

1956 Chinese officials create new style tai chi.

1970s Bruce Lee's martial arts movies make kung fu popular in the United States.

FIND OUT MORE

Books

Casey, Kevin. *Kung Fu.* Vero Beach, Fla.: Rourke, 1994.

Chen, Da. *Wandering Warrior.* New York: Delacorte Press, 2003.

Johnson, Nathan. *Kung Fu: Essential Tips, Drills, and Combat Techniques.*
Broomall, Pa.: Mason Crest Publishers, 2003.

McCully, Emily Arnold. *Beautiful Warrior: The Legend of the Nun's Kung Fu.*
New York: Scholastic Trade Books, 1998.

Olson, Stuart Alve. *Tai Chi for Kids: Move with the Animals.* Rochester, Vt.:
Bear & Co., 2001.

On the Web

Visit our home page for lots of links about kung fu and tai chi:
http://www.childsworld.com/links.html

NOTE TO PARENTS, TEACHERS, AND LIBRARIANS: We routinely check
our Web links to make sure they're safe, active sites—so encourage your
readers to check them out!

INDEX

ABOUT THE AUTHOR

Ann Heinrichs lives in Chicago, where she studies martial arts under Dr. Shi Cun Wu. She specializes in tai chi empty-hand and sword forms, with further training in broadsword, fan, Chang Chuan (Northern Shaolin Long Fist), Nan Chuan (Southern Fist), and kung fu sword. Ann is an award-winning competitor in regional and national tournaments, including the International Wushu-Gongfu Tournament. She is also the author of more than 100 nonfiction books for children and young adults. She once enjoyed a successful career as an advertising copywriter, but she finally quit her day job.